THE PLANETARY SOCIETY

T0109822

NEPTUNE

PLANET OF WIND AND ICE

Bruce Betts, PhD

Lerner Publications ◆ Minneapolis

THE PLANETS AND MOONS IN OUR SOLAR SYSTEM ARE OUT OF THIS WORLD. Some are hotter than an oven, and some are much colder than a freezer. Some are small and rocky, while others are huge and mostly made of gas. As you explore these worlds, you'll discover giant canyons, active volcanoes, strange kinds of ice, storms bigger than Earth, and much more.

The Planetary Society® empowers people around the world to advance space science and exploration. On behalf of The Planetary Society®, including our tens of thousands of members, here's wishing you the joy of discovery.

Onward,

Bill Nye

Bill Nye
CEO, The Planetary Society®

TABLE OF CONTENTS

CHAPTER 1

PLANET OF WIND AND ICE

Our solar system includes everything that goes around the Sun. There are eight planets. Neptune is the farthest planet from the Sun.

MEET PLANET NEPTUNE

Neptune is a little smaller than Uranus and much bigger than Earth. About fifty-eight Earths could fit inside Neptune.

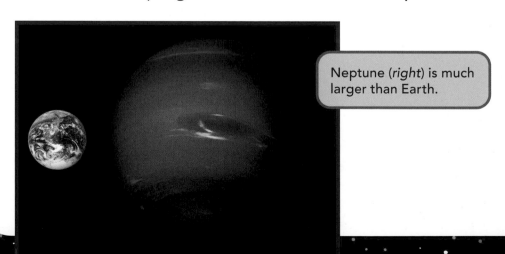

Neptune (*right*) is much larger than Earth.

Days are shorter on Neptune than on Earth. An Earth day is twenty-four hours. A Neptune day is about sixteen hours.

Years are much longer on Neptune than on Earth. A year is the time it takes a planet to go all the way around the Sun. One Earth year is about 365 days. One Neptune year is about 164 Earth years.

NEPTUNE FAST FACTS

Size	Could fit about fifty-eight Earths inside Neptune
Distance from the Sun	2.8 billion miles (4.5 billion km)
Length of day	About sixteen hours
Length of year	About 164 Earth years
Number of moons	At least fourteen

Neptune orbits, or goes around, the Sun far beyond the other planets. It is about thirty times farther from the Sun than Earth is.

Sunlight is almost one thousand times brighter at Earth than at Neptune. Much less sunlight means Neptune and its moons are much colder than Earth.

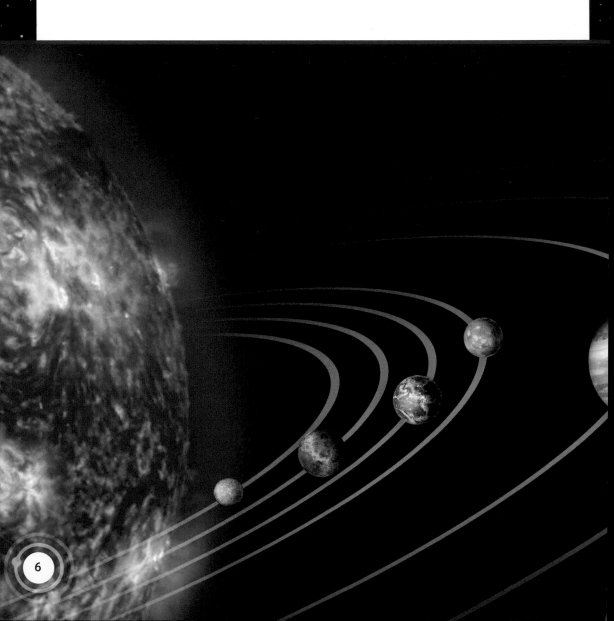

Far Away

What if you could drive a car straight from Earth to Neptune? It would take you about five thousand years to get there!

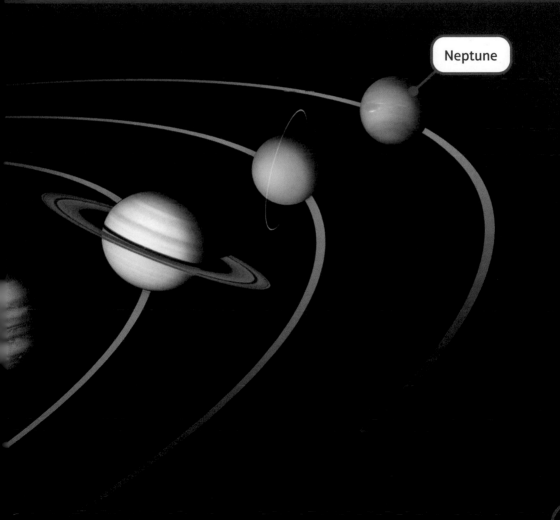

Neptune

GIANT AND ICE PLANETS

The four planets farthest from the Sun are called the outer or giant planets. They are Jupiter, Saturn, Uranus, and Neptune. They are much larger than Earth and the other inner, rocky planets.

Neptune and Uranus are also known as ice giants. They are mostly made of things that form ices. These include water, ammonia, and methane.

Left to right: Jupiter, Saturn, Uranus, and Neptune are the giant planets.

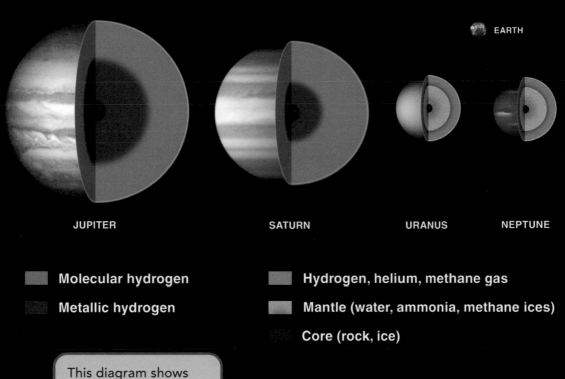

EARTH

JUPITER   SATURN   URANUS   NEPTUNE

Molecular hydrogen

Metallic hydrogen

Hydrogen, helium, methane gas

Mantle (water, ammonia, methane ices)

Core (rock, ice)

This diagram shows the inner layers of the giant planets.

The outer part of Neptune is all atmosphere. It is mostly made of hydrogen gas and some helium gas. It also has some methane. Methane makes the planet look blue.

Deeper down, Neptune has hot fluids. These include water, ammonia, and methane. There is likely a rocky core at the center of Neptune.

These two images taken by the Voyager 2 spacecraft show Neptune's rings.

All the giant planets have rings. But their rings are all different. Neptune's rings are very dark and hard to see. They are mostly made of dust. Neptune has at least five rings.

A statue of the Roman god Neptune

Neptune the God
Neptune is named after the Roman god of the same name. Neptune is the god of the sea. Planet Neptune's moons are named after Greek sea gods.

Neptune has at least fourteen moons. We could find more in the future.

Neptune (*behind*) and its moon Triton (*front*)

CHAPTER 2

FINDING STORMS AND MORE

You might be able to see Neptune in the night sky during some parts of the year. But you have to use a telescope to see Neptune. It's the only planet that you always need

People must use telescopes to see Neptune.

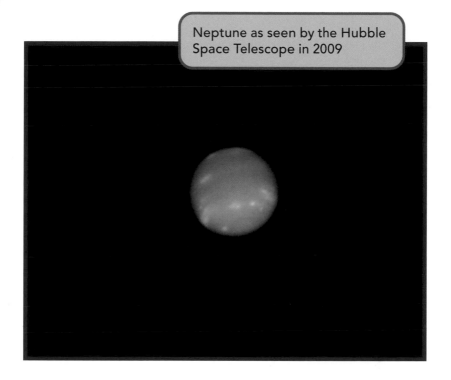

Neptune as seen by the Hubble Space Telescope in 2009

a telescope to see. Neptune looks like a small blue circle.

Scientists can see Neptune much better by using large telescopes on Earth and in space. They can track Neptune's clouds and dark spots. Some large telescopes can see some of Neptune's moons.

WINDS AND STORMS

The Voyager 2 spacecraft flew by Neptune in 1989. It was able to see many things in the atmosphere.

There were dark and light stripes. These stripes were winds blowing in different directions. There were also some circular storms and white clouds.

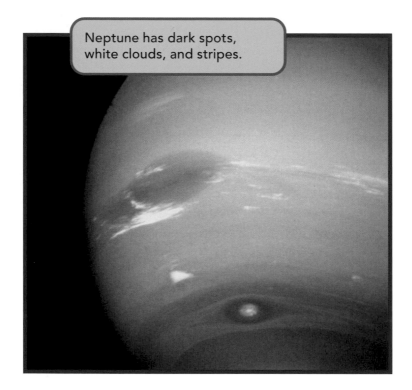

Neptune has dark spots, white clouds, and stripes.

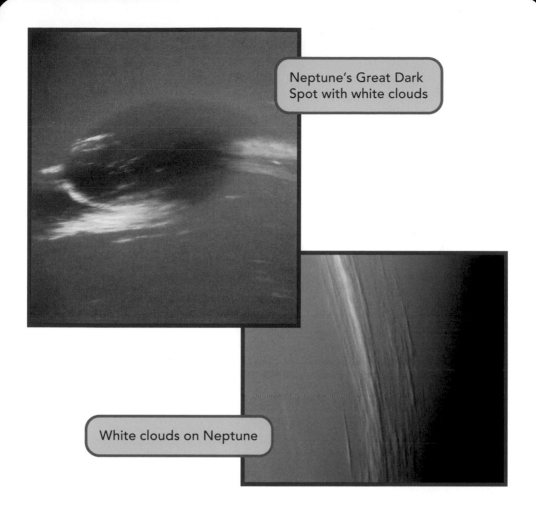

Neptune's Great Dark Spot with white clouds

White clouds on Neptune

Voyager 2 found the Great Dark Spot on Neptune. It was similar to Jupiter's Great Red Spot, another giant storm. The Great Dark Spot had white clouds.

Neptune has the fastest winds in the solar system. They are six times faster than the strongest hurricane winds on Earth. And they are four times faster than Earth's strongest tornado winds.

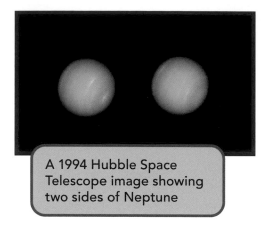

A 1994 Hubble Space Telescope image showing two sides of Neptune

We have built bigger and better Earth and space telescopes since Voyager 2 flew by Neptune. These new telescopes can see the planet in more detail. By 1994, the Hubble Space Telescope could see Neptune's storms. And it saw that the Great Dark Spot was gone.

The Hubble Space Telescope

We have seen many storms on Neptune. Telescopes have seen at least five new dark spots. They all go away within a few years.

There are also white clouds. They are likely made of methane ice. The clouds come and go like Neptune's storms.

The 2018 image on the left shows Neptune with a dark spot and white clouds. The 2020 image on the right shows the same dark spot without white clouds, and a new dark spot.

Neptune's rings with ring arcs

THE RINGS

Scientists have found five main rings around Neptune. They are very dark and made of dust and some ice. Some are narrow. Others are wide and harder to see.

Neptune's outer ring has ring arcs. A ring arc is when more dust is in some parts of the ring than others. Only Neptune's ring has them.

We don't know how the ring arcs stay in place. But the small moon Galatea may be the reason. It orbits just inside the ring. The pull of its gravity may keep the arcs in place.

Ring Names

Neptune's rings are named after scientists. The scientists were part of the discovery or early studies of Neptune.

A 2022 infrared (a kind of light we can't see) image showing the best view of Neptune's rings since 1989

Neptune's rings are faint and far away from our planet. That makes it hard to take pictures of them from Earth. Since 2022, the James Webb Space Telescope has made it easier for us to see them.

MOONS

Neptune has fourteen known moons. All the moons except Triton are small. They come in many shapes.

Triton is by far the largest moon of Neptune. It is the seventh-largest moon in the solar system.

Proteus, one of Neptune's moons

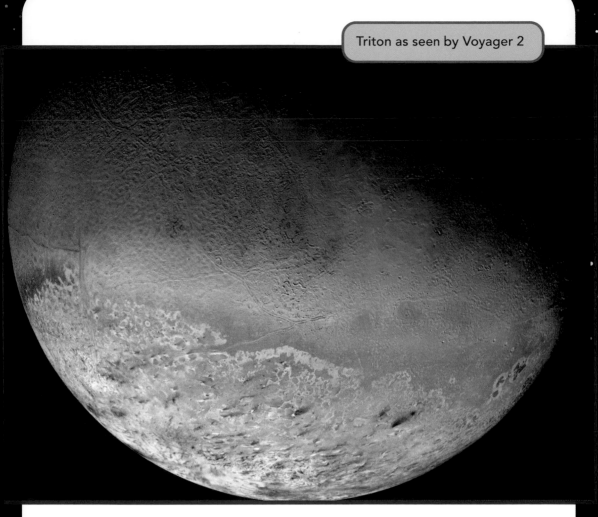

Triton is the only large moon in the solar system that doesn't go around its planet in the same direction the planet spins. That is a clue that Triton likely did not form with Neptune. Neptune may have pulled in Triton when it passed too close.

Like Neptune, Triton is far from the Sun and gets very cold. Triton's surface is around −391°F (−235°C). Water ice and strange ices such as methane ice and nitrogen ice freeze on the surface.

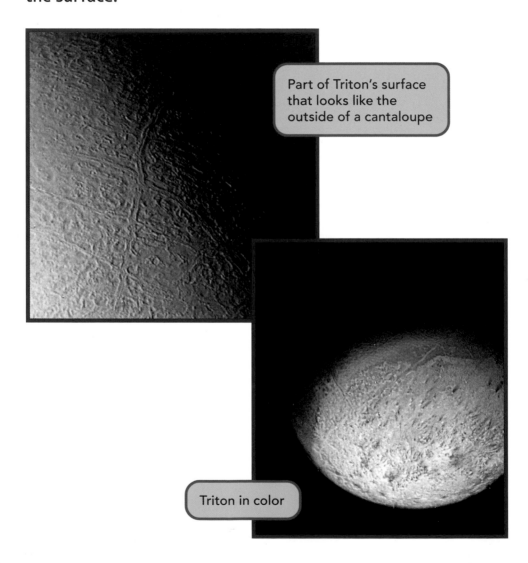

Part of Triton's surface that looks like the outside of a cantaloupe

Triton in color

Triton has a surface unlike anywhere else in the solar system. Part of Triton looks like the outside of a cantaloupe. Other parts have dark and light spots.

Some areas are volcanic plains. On Earth, they are made of rock that came out of a volcano. On Triton, they are made of ices that flowed out of a volcano and then froze.

Triton has a very thin atmosphere that has nitrogen gas. There is also wind. There are wind streaks of dark material on part of Triton's surface.

The moon also has active geysers. They shoot up a mix of liquid nitrogen, methane, and dust. The geysers can shoot the mix up to 5 miles (8 km) high! Wind may then blow it miles away.

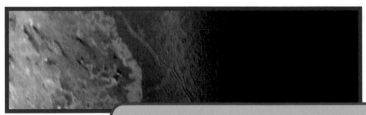

This edited color image shows the part of Triton that looks like the outside of a cantaloupe (*right*) and wind streaks of the mix that comes from the geysers (*left*).

CHAPTER 3

EXPLORING NEPTUNE

We use spacecraft to study the planets up close. Voyager 2 is the only spacecraft to have visited Neptune. That is because Neptune is so far away from Earth. It takes a lot of time and money to build and send spacecraft there.

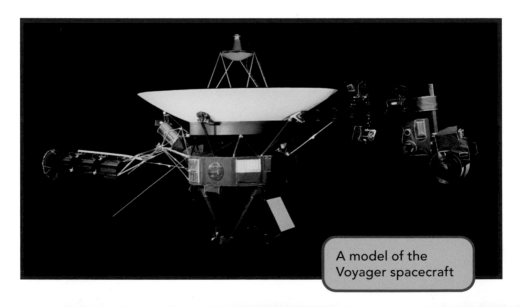

A model of the Voyager spacecraft

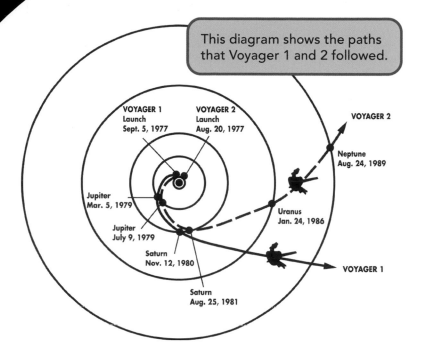

This diagram shows the paths that Voyager 1 and 2 followed.

VOYAGER 1
Launch
Sept. 5, 1977

VOYAGER 2
Launch
Aug. 20, 1977

VOYAGER 2

Neptune
Aug. 24, 1989

Jupiter
Mar. 5, 1979

Uranus
Jan. 24, 1986

Jupiter
July 9, 1979

Saturn
Nov. 12, 1980

VOYAGER 1

Saturn
Aug. 25, 1981

MISSION TO NEPTUNE

Voyager 2 launched in 1977. It visited Neptune and the other giant planets. This was called the Grand Tour. All our close-up views of Neptune, its moons, and its rings come from Voyager 2.

Voyager 2 was able to visit all the giant planets because the planets were in just the right places. That happens only once every 175 years. By launching when it did, Voyager 2 was able to use the gravity of each planet to help change its course to reach the next planet.

A Long Trip

Voyager 2 traveled at tens of thousands of miles per hour. But it still took twelve years to reach Neptune.

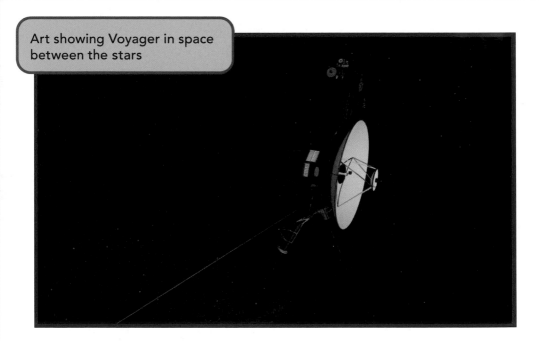

Art showing Voyager in space between the stars

THE FUTURE

Voyager 2 and its twin Voyager 1 still work and are billions of miles away. They are the farthest human-made objects from Earth. They have enough speed that they will leave the solar system and never come back.

No spacecraft mission is currently planned to go to Neptune. But there will likely be another mission to Neptune in the future.

The good news is our telescopes have gotten better. We can keep studying Neptune. And we can see how the planet changes over time.

Triton

Galatea
Naiad
Thalassa
Despina
Proteus
Larissa

Neptune, its rings, and some of its moons are seen in this 2022 infrared image.

There will be more to learn and solve about Neptune in the coming years. And that's only one of the eight planets! Enjoy your journey through the solar system.

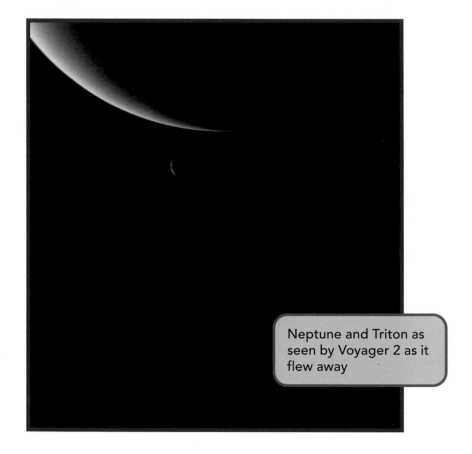

Neptune and Triton as seen by Voyager 2 as it flew away

A Titan IIIE-Centaur rocket launches in 1977 with Voyager 2.

Glossary

atmosphere: the gases surrounding a planet, moon, or other body

core: the center of a planet or moon

day: the time it takes a planet to spin around and go from noon to noon. One Earth day is about twenty-four hours.

geyser: a spring that shoots a stream of hot water, steam, or mud into the air. On Triton, geysers shoot a mix of liquid nitrogen, methane, and dust.

planet: a big, round, ball-shaped object that only goes around the Sun. Our solar system has eight planets. A planet does not have anything close to the same size near its orbit.

spacecraft: a vehicle or object made for travel in outer space

year: the time it takes a planet to go all the way around the Sun. One Earth year is about 365 days.

Learn More

Betts, Bruce, PhD. *Uranus: The Sideways Planet*. Minneapolis: Lerner Publications, 2025.

Britannica Kids: Neptune
    https://kids.britannica.com/kids/article/Neptune/353526

Lawrence, Ellen. *Neptune: The Stormiest Planet*. Chicago: Sequoia Kids Media, 2022.

Mazzarella, Kerri. *Neptune*. Coral Springs, FL: Seahorse, 2023.

NASA Space Place: All about Neptune
    https://spaceplace.nasa.gov/all-about-neptune/en/

The Planetary Society: Neptune, Planet of Wind and Ice
    https://www.planetary.org/worlds/neptune

INDEX

PHOTO ACKNOWLEDGMENTS

Image credits: The Planetary Society, p. 2; NASA/Wikimedia Commons (PD), pp. 4, 8, 25; NASA/JPL, pp. 6–7, 10 (top), 14, 15 (top and bottom), 18, 20, 22 (left and right), 23, 28–29; NASA/Lunar And Planetary Institute, p. 9; Art Images/Getty Images, p. 10 (bottom); NASA/JPL/USGS, pp. 11, 21; JasonDoiy/Getty Images, p. 12; NASA, ESA, and M. Showalter (SETI Institute), p. 13; NASA/JPL/STScI, p. 16 (top); AP Photo/ NASA, p. 16 (bottom); NASA, ESA, and A. Simon (NASA Goddard Space Flight Center), and M. Wong and A. Hsu (University of California, Berkeley), p. 17 (left); NASA, ESA, STScI, M.H. Wong (University of California, Berkeley) and L.A. Sromovsky and P.M. Fry (University of Wisconsin–Madison), p. 17 (right); NASA, ESA, CSA, STScI, p. 19; NASA/ Hulton Archive/Getty Images, p. 24; NASA/JPL-Caltech, p. 26; NASA, ESA, CSA, STScI, p. 27. Design elements: Anna Frajtova/Shutterstock; Baac3nes/Getty Images; Elena Kryulena/Shutterstock; Sergey Balakhnichev/Getty Images.
Cover: NASA/JPL-Caltech/Björn Jónsson/The Planetary Society.

FOR MY SONS, DANIEL AND KEVIN, AND FOR ALL THE MEMBERS OF THE PLANETARY SOCIETY®

Lerner Publications Company
An imprint of Lerner Publishing Group, Inc.
241 First Avenue North
Minneapolis, MN 55401 USA

For reading levels and more information, look up this title at www.lernerbooks.com.

Main body text set in Aptifer Sans LT Pro. Typeface provided by Linotype AG.

Editor: Brianna Kaiser **Designer:** Mary Ross
Lerner team: Connie Kuhnz

Library of Congress Cataloging-in-Publication Data

Names: Betts, Bruce (PhD), author.
Title: Neptune : planet of wind and ice / Bruce Betts, PhD.
Description: Minneapolis, MN : Lerner Publications, [2025] | Series: Exploring our solar system with the Planetary Society | Includes bibliographical references and index. | Audience: Ages 7–10 | Audience: Grades 2–3 | Summary: "Neptune, the farthest planet from our Sun, is a dark and windy planet. Young space fans discover Neptune's rings, moons, and ice through bright photos and colorful diagrams"— Provided by publisher.
Identifiers: LCCN 2023049544 (print) | LCCN 2023049545 (ebook) | ISBN 9798765626887 (library binding) | ISBN 9798765628652 (paperback) | ISBN 9798765633328 (epub)
Subjects: LCSH: Neptune (Planet)—Juvenile literature.
Classification: LCC QB691 .B48 2025 (print) | LCC QB691 (ebook) | DDC 523.48—dc23/eng/20231122

LC record available at https://lccn.loc.gov/2023049544
LC ebook record available at https://lccn.loc.gov/2023049545

Manufactured in the United States of America
1-1010104-52019-2/21/2024